CONVERSATIONS WITH A SERVANT OF GOD

Lessons in Spiritual Guidance

FANELLA SAMPSON

Fanella C. Sampson

DEDICATION

This book is dedicated to the glory of God through Jesus Christ, my LORD and Savior. He has given me life and sustained me through the years of trial and temptation to be alive today as a testimony and a witness to His truthfulness, faithfulness, and steadfastness. And to all those who will be inspired and touched by this book to worship Him continually in Spirit and in Truth.

CONTENTS

PREFACE

I am giving glory to God for allowing me to see my 75th birthday. If you read my first book How Great Thou Art, you will appreciate that my life, being fraught by many and varied temptations and trials, is only by the grace of God. I should not be alive today. God has saved me from many a death sentence through miscellaneous intrigues, tests, and trials. And so, I give him all the glory.

Over the past 7 years, God's extraordinary hand of salvation and deliverance has been manifested in my life mainly through my interactions with my church family, and invariably through my relationship and constant fellowship with Apostle Kevin Etta. By prayers on the basis of direct revelation from God or on the basis of his ongoing interpretative conversations with me about the substance, meanings, and implications of my own dreams and visions, God has created a theater where my challenges have been addressed and I have continued to enjoy a meaningful life to His praise and glory.

It is in this light that I am sharing just a snippet of this interpretative conversation with this servant of God, in the hopes that the explanations, lessons, and insights there might be edifying to some and helpful to others in understanding the ways of the Spirit of God and how He partners with our spirit in the war against elemental forces of evil that swirl around us to give us victory in Christ Jesus our LORD.

Fanella Christiana Sampson
May, 2023

ONE

A VISION OF COMFORT AND ASSURANCE DESPITE BAD ACTORS IN MY LIFE
(February 2020)

I woke very early and as usual laid in bed and was ordered to pray for Apostle and Jane Doe while awake and I did. Then continued singing my religious songs then dosed off again. This time we were in a house where I have changed the toilet earlier on to one of a higher height (i.e., to a higher, raised-level, commode). When I entered the house, I noticed that it was replaced by another one (i.e., changed back to the lower-level toilet/commode) by two men. So, as a guest in the house I went to ask Apostle if he gave the okay for them to do so. I was so mad and told Apostle that these men were thieves that's how they rob other customers. They thought that I will not know. While inside the door closed. This time we were in my grandma's house in Bonthe. I wanted to surprise Apostle with breakfast, so I decided to cook him something. As I was about to do this, an American lady volunteered to help me do the cooking. There was flour everywhere and I was not satisfied with her cooking. Suddenly, a tall American man and Jane Doe appeared. I wanted to go to the other room where I keep the plates to serve Apostle food. Before I could enter the room, I saw (through the closed door, somehow) Apostle was sitting in the room and bright light shone around him. So, I said: "now I know for sure that Apostle is different".

I knocked on the room door and we communicated (through the closed door) and I told Apostle that I just saw him in the room even while he was behind a closed door. Apostle told me that I should go with him to a shelter for battered women where they are cared for. Instead of Apostle eating, he preferred one of the battered women who was sheltering there at the time to eat first. Jane Doe was not pleased with this and snatched the fork from her. While this drama was going on, the American man made his way to sit by Apostle on the table and I was not able to serve Apostle and I woke up.

A lot of times visions and dreams open up in layers, doorways and portals of realization and awareness (of our changed or evolved situation and circumstances) as we peer deeper in the realm. Or simply as we awake from one dream, pray, and then drift back to sleep. Oftentimes this drifting back to sleep after having been awakened by a dream or a voice asking us to pray propels us into another layer, or into the interpretative theater or context of the dream where other layers, portals or doorways of the revelation open up and manifest themselves in the changing kaleidoscope of our dream or visionary state. We are able to see further and glean more knowledge or instruction about what it is God is trying to show or tell us, and in different ways, shapes and forms.

In Daniel 8:1-3 we see somewhat of an example of this as it happened to Daniel. It reads:

"1 In the third year of the reign of king Belshazzar a vision appeared unto me, even unto me, Daniel, after that which appeared unto me at the first. 2 And I saw in the vision (i.e., the vision began to unfold before me); now it was so, that when I saw, I was in Shushan the palace (i.e., as I peered into the vision I realized the theater that

TWO

VISION OF NATIONAL CHAOS
(April 2020)

"I had this vision between 2:30 a.m. and 3:00 a.m. We were in this building (like a church). On the right side of the building on the television I saw a national leader on the microphone talking but his speech was not clear. So, when I looked at him, he looked like someone without teeth. Suddenly, there was an uncontrollable fire and he and all that were around him started running for shelter. I saw all the tall buildings burning down on the left and on the right. We were in the unfolded placed me in Shushan, the palace…), which is in the province of Elam; and I saw in the vision, and I was by the river Ulai (i.e., the more I peered into the vision the theater is evolving more and I realize that it has placed me by the Ulai river). 3 Then I lifted up mine eyes, and saw, and, behold… (i.e., as I become more intrigued by the vision and peer around me, something extraordinary evolves or appears before me…).

Oftentimes, dreams, visions, and revelations are progressive in how they unfold and layer themselves out until we arrive at the ground zero of the revelation; i.e., the spot where the core message or instruction will be presented or communicated to us. And the intervening and preceding curtains and doorways that lead up to this ground zero may (or may not) always be significant. But the core message (the ground zero) of the vision is where we hear or see what is critical. It is why we are brought into the vision to begin with.

I will divide this revelation up into different parts to make it easier to breakdown.

Part 1

"I woke very early and as usual laid in bed and was ordered to pray for Apostle and Jane Doe while awake and I did. Then continued singing my religious songs then dosed off again. This time we were in a house..."

So, in this revelation, I awoke from a dream or other experience with the instruction to pray for the Apostle and Jane Doe. And after I prayed, I sang songs of worship softly while I lay in bed – until I drifted off again. And then I find myself back in the original revelation, albeit in a different layer or theater of the vision, where things are displayed with more clarity, and the situation for which I had been asked to pray for Apostle and Jane Doe appeared in more vivid detail for my spiritual interaction and education within the revelation. As I peer into the revelation (like Daniel in Daniel 8:1-3), I am able to see and participate in the revelatory outplay and enactment and advance deeper into the vision's core or ground zero. There are times when a revelation will have more than one core, as in a core within a core –each successive core only unfolding when one has traversed the one preceding and performed the interaction or derived the education that was inherent before it transpires. In this case, I am moving into the first layer of the revelation.

Part 2

"We were in a house where I have changed the toilet earlier on to one of a higher height (i.e., to a higher, raised-level, commode). When I entered the house, I noticed that it was replaced by another one (i.e., changed back to a lower-level toilet/commode) by two men. So, as a guest in the house I went to ask Apostle if he gave the okay for them to do so. I was so mad and told Apostle that these men were thieves that's how they rob other customers. They thought that I will not know…"

So, a toilet is a process of washing or cleaning oneself, of performing ablutions and grooming oneself —so that you are constantly flushing out waste, toxins, and death from your system through an established process and routine that is safe and sanitary. In this revelation it shows that the toilet had been replaced with a better quality and more comfortable version, and this representation (i.e., of the raised toilet) shows that God has been answering the prayers of the church regarding my general health and wellbeing, which is in a good state given my activity in the church where I was receiving Grace. But as is so often the case, when the enemy saw that I was benefitting from the Grace of God he attempted to undo what God had done (hence, the two men had gone and reversed what God had already done). I saw this in the vision (I wasn't supposed to see, but God brought me to this layer or theater within the vision to expose their evil activity), I had alerted

Apostle (who, in real life, has been the one praying for me and has been my mentor). In my protestation to Apostle, I defined accurately the character of these evil elements as being "thieves" who "rob" the unsuspecting.

A couple of Scriptures shed light and illuminate this experience.

"24 Another parable put he forth unto them, saying, The kingdom of heaven is likened unto a man which sowed good seed in his field: 25 But while men slept, his enemy came and sowed tares among the wheat, and went his way. 26 But when the blade was sprung up, and brought forth fruit, then appeared the tares also. 27 So the servants of the householder came and said unto him, Sir, didst not thou sow good seed in thy field? from whence then hath it tares? 28 He said unto them, An enemy hath done this. The servants said unto him, Wilt thou then that we go and gather them up?" (Matthew 13:24-28).

In the Scripture, we are shown that oftentimes when God is working to bring about salvation, the enemy is also working to undo God's work in our lives.

Another Scripture in John 10:10 clearly identifies these evil elements with the same description that I used in my revelation by calling them "thieves".

"The thief does not come except to steal, and to kill, and to destroy. I have come that they may have life, and that they may have it more abundantly."

The remedy here is prayer, hence I challenged Apostle (in the vision) by making him to know that certain evil elements were trying to undo the good work that God has being doing in my life. And that he should help me pray and work against them to the glory of God.

Part 3

"While inside the door closed. This time we were in my grandma's house in Bonthe. I wanted to surprise Apostle with breakfast, so I decided to cook him something. As I was about to do this an American lady volunteered to help me do the cooking. There was flour everywhere and I was not satisfied with her cooking. Suddenly, a tall American man and Jane Doe appeared. I wanted to go to the other room where I keep the plates to serve Apostle food. Before I could enter the room, I saw (through the closed door, somehow) Apostle was sitting in the room and bright light shone around him. So, I said: "now I know for sure that Apostle is different".

I knocked on the room door and we

communicated (through the closed door) and I told Apostle that I just saw him in the room even while he was behind a closed door. Apostle told me that I should go with him to a shelter for battered women where they are cared for. Instead of Apostle eating, he preferred one of the battered women who was sheltering there at the time to eat first. Jane Doe was not pleased with this and snatched the fork from her. While this drama was going on, the American man made his way to sit by Apostle on the table and I was not able to serve Apostle and I woke up."

In this section of the revelation, I am still traveling through the vision, from one theater to another –and, in this case, from one core to another. This theater is very elaborate and expansive, and there is much being shown to me here. God is speaking words of comfort to me, given the challenges I am facing which He has revealed are coming from some evil elements trying to undo the good work that I have been enjoying through the grace of my church and prayers from the Apostle.

I am trying to give Apostle breakfast. This is significant. Apostle is constantly praying and fussing over me and my welfare, and God is trying to comfort me by showing me how much He loves and cares for me by making this kind of extraordinary provision for me. And so, I am exercised in my mind and my spirit about how I can reward Apostle for his work and to keep him motivated to continue praying for me. "Breakfast" means just that: "breaking a fast"; i.e., a relief or provision we give to someone to break their fast or to replenish them after their fasting and/or prayer for us. And this is true: I always think of what to do for Apostle for his love and care. But, as the vision bore out, no matter what I do for him, he is less interested (though extremely appreciative) and more focused on converting and refocusing all his energies to the Ministry work. Despite the fact a lot of people who come around him only want to take from him, and not give back --and others with ulterior motives engage in in-fighting and rivalry among themselves --he remains focused on his mission and his ministry, not wanting any reward for himself but only for others.

The comfort and lesson for me in this vision was that despite my challenges and trials, God has made adequate provision for my safety and protection, and He has put the right people in my life to shepherd and guide me onward.

middle of it all. Immediately, I held the hands of two children and started walking to escape with them. Two female relatives (one of whom is deceased) were with me. I asked the one who is now a decedent for the whereabouts of her sister (who suddenly had disappeared) and she replied that her sister was waiting for someone (i.e., she had stayed behind). So, we left her behind while we continued walking, us, and the kids together. Eventually, we saw that we were surrounded by sea and while walking through to the East, I noticed that we were walking (wading) through shallow water while I saw many people in the sea swimming trying to escape from the intense burning fire. Suddenly, I woke up."

The vision's interpretation and how it was resolved for me is rendered below with some editing, being divided into four parts (1 through 4) to make it easier to follow.

1. "We were in this building (like church). On the right side of the building on the television, I saw a national leader on the microphone talking but his speech was not clear. So, when I looked at him, he looked like someone without teeth."

2. "Suddenly, there was an uncontrollable fire and he and all that were around him started running for shelter. I saw all the

tall buildings burning down on the left and on the right. We were in the middle of all."

3. "Immediately, I held the hands of two children and started walking to escape with them. Two adult acquaintances were with me. I asked the first one while we walked about the second one, and she told me that the second adult acquaintance was waiting for someone. So, we left her behind.

4. "While the first adult acquaintance, the two children, and I, were walking, we saw that we were surrounded by sea and while walking through to the East, I noticed that we were walking in shallow water, while I saw many people in the sea swimming trying to escape from the intense burning fire. Suddenly, I woke up."

Part 1

Obviously, this is a message for the Church and God begins by revealing something about the national leader: his speech being "not clear" speaks to his policies not pursuing or adhering to clarity, truth, and right and proper judgement and thereby causing widespread confusion. His teeth being either broken, eroded or non-existent, speak to him being a wicked and callous man, a liar and a deceiver who cannot be trusted.

To help you get a grip on this, below are some Scriptures that mirror the imagery of broken or missing teeth and what they generally point to in spiritual realities:

Proverbs 25:19
"Putting confidence in an unreliable person
In times of trouble is like chewing with
A broken tooth or walking on a lame foot."

Psalm 112:10
"The wicked will see it and be vexed,
He will gnash his teeth and melt away;
The desire of the wicked will perish."

Psalm 58:6
"O God, shatter their teeth in their mouth;
Break out the fangs of the young lions,
O Lord."

Psalm 3:7
"Arise, O Lord; save me, O my God!
For You have smitten all my enemies on the cheek; You have shattered the teeth of the wicked."

Part 2

It is clear to see that the mishandling of the pandemic from the start –beginning with serial denials of its existence and miscellaneous obfuscations about the virus itself –resulted in ill-preparation for its devastating effects at the national and the state levels. The manifest and rampant missteps, misinformation, deflections, and policy somersaults of those in authority allowed the health crisis to metastasize into a full-blown pandemic. Discordant tunes and messaging between federal and state agencies and authorities, politicizing of the COVID preparedness and response strategies at each and every level of governance –and the lack of a unified, coherent, national policy to combat the pandemic --put our nation, our economy and our healthcare systems under serious threat and stress and risked the lives and health of hundreds of thousands. Hence, the nation is "on fire", if you will, with a crisis that is seemingly uncontrollable (but God will control it).

And it is this crisis, among other things, that will see to the exit and departure of this national leader and the disappointment of his sponsors and supporters.

It is important to note that this vision was given in April of 2020 at the beginning of the pandemic season when there was widespread panic, confusion, and uncertainty not just nationally but globally about the future. In addition, this was a field day for conspiracy theorists and purveyors of misinformation and disinformation, many of such persons being found in the religious space. In fact, and this is extremely sad, certain elements of the established and mainstream Christian churches were at the forefront of the denialism that exacerbated the national COVID crisis and were also chief sponsors of leaders at the national and state levels that propagated denialism and undermined legitimate efforts of healthcare agencies to carry out remediation steps to mitigate and control the COVID outbreak.

This denialism extended to the political space and threatened to affect the outcome of the 2020 elections and the smooth handover of power. Several established and celebrated pastors, prophets and apostles made wild and outlandish prescriptions about the outcomes of the elections and of the outcomes of the certification processes (after the elections had been concluded) in ways that threatened the very fabric and stability of American democracy (but which were eventually disproved and shamed).

However, in and through it all, the words of this vision and the interpretation (altogether, tantamount to a prophecy from the LORD) were a source of comfort and assurance to our church, because we rested in the knowledge that: "[The] decision is by the decree of the watchers, And the sentence by the word of the holy ones, In order that the living may know That the Most High rules in the kingdom of men, Gives it to whomever He will, And sets over it the lowest of men" (Daniel 4:17, NKJV).

Parts 3 and 4

God has made a provision, in accordance with Psalm 91, to protect, secure and sustain His people —if they will trust in Him like little children. And remain obedient to Him and seek Him daily versus seek other counselors and advisors. So that some that could've been forgone cases will be saved and secured (i.e., the 'deceased' was the sister who was saved), whilst others who could've been safe and secure —but like Lot's wife looked back to the world, its customs, its fear and its acceptance —will be lost (in the vision, the other sister who was supposedly safe was ultimately lost because she allowed herself to be drawn away by distractions from people, etc.). Remember the Scripture which says:

"29 And everyone who has left houses or brothers or sisters or father or mother or wife or children or lands, for My name's sake, shall receive a hundredfold, and inherit eternal life. 30 BUT MANY WHO ARE FIRST WILL BE LAST, AND THE LAST FIRST." (Matthew 19:29-30).

God's children (in accordance with Psalm 91) will pass through this flood in shallow water (i.e., they shall pass through safely) onward to the East (i.e., to the sunrise, the promise of a new day; promise of deliverance and salvation from this crisis). Whilst many others, some of whom trust in the world and its systems, will struggle, and be consumed by the deep waters (i.e., the confusion this crisis has thrown up in all its layers and forms).

While we continue to heed and take the advice of public health agencies and authorities, remain focused and obedient to the faith, and seek the LORD daily. He is your salvation not man, not social media, not hearsay, not conspiracy theories. But the LORD.

In Amos 3:7 we are told: "Surely the Sovereign LORD does nothing without revealing his plan to his servants the prophets" (NIV). This was a vision the LORD sent because He knew there was a reliable mechanism for the interpretation of His words which were given to comfort and assure the Saints in our church of His watchful care (this vision and the interpretation was shared within our church at the time).

He is ever mindful of the confusion and trepidation that pervades the land in times of crises, with different groups –political, religious, and commercial --competing to saturate the airwaves and communications streams and to influence people one way or the other —or just to cause mass hysteria and panic for ungodly reasons.

THREE

A VISION OF CONTINUING HEALING BY THE GRACE OF GOD
(September 2019)

"I was in a house that was undergoing repairs and I was cleaning. Outside I saw some men cleaning the house. In their midst there stood a fair skinned young man. I was curious, and so I asked the men who he was and was told that he is a millionaire. However, he did not look like one.

"Suddenly, I was in a crowd of people and this young man saw me and wanted to talk to me. I observed that He was constantly looking at me.

However, his guards did not allow him to approach me. I was with another woman and was confiding in her that the young man has an interest in me, but I have doubts about him. While this lady and I walked together and talked, I saw two other women who were eavesdropping on our conversation --and appeared to be getting jealous about what I was saying (i.e., about the fair skinned man's interest in me). While all of us were standing, two of the millionaire's guards came towards us with a fresh papaya and envelopes of money and letter to give me. But I told them to hand them to the women who were with me.

"On our way going, I saw a person of great stature on a horse. This royal emissary spoke to me and asked if I received the things the millionaire sent to me. I said yes. The emissary said that in one of the envelopes I was asked to send my picture so that it can be given to the king, the millionaire's father. Then I woke up."

The vision's rendering was given in this way…

The "house" you were in was in a poor state and needing repair, refurbishing, and cleansing. In this vision, the house is your body, the temple of your spirit, and your physical body is in a poor state of health and needing repair and healing, given your revolving or rotational state of on-again, off-again virility, buoyancy and well-being.

And what is happening with the activity around the house with the people cleaning and assisting with the repairs, etc., is the counterpart similitude of the regime of prayers that have been ongoing on your behalf, due to other revelation that evidenced the fact your body is requiring constant regenerative stimulation and refreshing from the LORD. And this is what you see. You should have died years ago but it is the LORD that is sustaining you through this regenerative treatment to be able to survive until this day. And this is why the Heavenly emissary demanded your picture: this is a similitude to convey the fact that the Father in Heaven is constantly renewing your image to maintain and sustain you upon the earth.

The young fair-skinned man is the LORD, who sometimes appears in a way that does not tell of His great stature. This is how He appeared when he walked the earth, and oftentimes in visions and revelations he chooses to appear the same way.

It is clear (from the vision) to see that the LORD is very interested in you, but sometimes He is restricted from coming close to you because you are not always in the best of company. Not everyone with whom you associate is wishing you well. Hence, the jealousy of the women around you and the plotting to withhold your blessings from you, and also influencing you to either deny your blessing or forfeit them through ignorance.

"Look! I stand at the door and knock. If you hear my voice and open the door, I will come in, and we will share a meal together as friends." (Revelation 3:20, NLT).

We see from that Scripture that oftentimes, while it is the LORD's wish to come close to us, He cannot if we do not create the circumstances that will allow Him to do so.

Isaiah 59:2 (NIV) also states:
"But your iniquities have separated you from your God; your sins have hidden his face from you, so that he will not hear."

So, again, sometimes our decisions and associations prevent the LORD from coming close to us to accomplish His will of healing and salvation. We need to separate ourselves from what is unholy, be they persons or things.

2 Corinthians 6:17, NKJV, says:
"Therefore "Come out from among them And be separate, says the Lord. Do not touch what is unclean, And I will receive you.""

The host of Heaven have come to attend to your health and cleanse and purge you of poisons and toxins that have afflicted you by witchcraft and miscellaneous kinds of evil.
They gave you fresh papaya, which is a

similitude of serum or plasma to rebuild and regenerate your damaged tissues, sinews and other body elements and organs. You also received money and further messages (the letters). May you walk in obedience to receive all that the LORD has for you, and so that they will bear fruit in you. You need greater obedience in your walk with God and in recalibrating your relations with others so that you will not hinder the work of God in your life.

Again, this is a message of comfort and warning. You need to make adjustments in the ways you associate with certain persons, community, and family. This is a command from God.

FOUR

A NEW DIRECTION

I had this vision where Apostle was in a building but not his house and he was working at resurfacing and repainting the dirty walls, and so I also began to help with repairs to the ceiling. There were helpers who came to help Apostle with the work, and I was glad. After a while it appears that I was with a white man, and we were in a room with the owner of the room. Next, one of the divine helpers went with me out of the building. I saw a forest on my left and a lake like on my right-hand. I saw people standing in the lake with only their heads above water, but the rest of their body was immersed below the water's surface, and I was told that they are crab hunting. We passed them and suddenly we were being chased by dogs or some forest animals, so we escaped and came back into the house. I saw many people gathered and they were holding a meeting. And there were other familiar faces that I saw. Apostle brought in two new old-style classic typewriters and other office supplies trying to set up the office. It reminded me of my work in the early days with something similar. Also, in the building that you were painting you asked for those who will covenant with the LORD to see His righteousness established, and I was one of those who signified a willingness to covenant with the LORD in the work that He would do in that house. While still in this building I saw your son Daniel come in singing a very unknown religious song that is not familiar to me, but he was helped with other young people singing. The song was a beautiful song.

The interpretation of this vision was rendered in this way:

The Ministry was undergoing some radical changes and shifts. God is working to bring about a new direction and to mobilize new energies, competencies, capacities, and abilities. There would also be new officers ordained into different functions in the church (all of this happened within the space of a few months). This is why Apostle was working along with divine helpers to renovate the church.

Again, as was pointed out earlier, oftentimes we gravitate and float through different doorways and portals of a revelation to enter its core, or a succession of cores, where the same, or expanded or different truth is unfolded and unveiled – similar to how a node in a graphical representation or organization's "org tree" structure is exploded to reveal a network of connected sub-nodes, sub-orgs or sub-depts each with its own detailed definitions and characteristics. So, in this vision, the visioner or watcher is taken from one level to another to see the progression of God's purpose in and through the church (which is the focus and object of the vision).

Moving into a layer where there is a forest on one side and a lake on another, and having to be aware of the threat of wild beasts on the one hand (i.e. wild dogs, snakes and scorpions; i.e. demonic and misc. evil forces, entities and resistance) and on the other hand have an awareness equivalent to those who hunt for crabs (crabs are creatures that can live and crawl between land and water, so they represent spiritual beings that hide inside and pass as human beings in churches, amongst brethren, so-called ministers of God, etc.) reveals that the church will have heightened discernment of spirits to identify and expose false spirits, false ministers, false teachings, and hidden demonic activity in people who traverse our space or with whom we interact in prayer and fellowship, etc.

This mandate from God is to be manifested concurrently with the boldness and utterance given to the church to utter and deliver the mysteries of God through His word, hence the paraphernalia of the classic old-style typewriter being brought into an office setting within the house (i.e., the original and unadulterated Word of Truth and Light will be propagated in and through the assembly). All of this to be accomplished in and through the power of the Holy Spirit who will also invigorate and actuate a new direction through the Youth Ministry in the church.

There is also a covenant that Apostle called into play for any and all who would dedicate and rededicate themselves to the work of the Ministry, so that they would be sealed into the promises and the Grace that was being released to effectuate the vision. This is like what Moses did in Exodus 32:26:

"Moses stood in the entrance of the camp, and said, "Whoever is on the LORD's side—come to me!" And all the sons of Levi gathered themselves together to him."

Joshua did the same thing in Joshua 24:15:

"And if it seem evil unto you to serve the LORD, choose you this day whom ye will serve; whether the gods which your fathers served that were on the other side of the flood, or the gods of the Amorites, in whose land ye dwell: but as for me and my house, we will serve the LORD."

This vision was a message of comfort, wisdom, and direction for the Ministry, to redirect their gaze to a new path that the LORD was bringing in focus and into being in the collective experience of the brethren.

FIVE

PREPARED FOR THE WORK OF GOD

God's way of delivering instruction to us is granularly, incrementally, in an ascending gradient and crescendo, based on our attention, adherence and obedience to His words. This is why visions, dreams, and spiritual revelation are so layered, oftentimes repetitive and iterative, in cycles and revolutions of scene upon scene, portal after portal, and core after core.

Isaiah 28:10 bears this trademark pattern and flow by which revelation is unfolded and unveiled to us.

"He is trying to teach us letter by letter, line by line, lesson by lesson." (Good News Translation).

"He tells us everything over and over— one line at a time, one line at a time, a little here, and a little there!" (NLT).

So, God's instructions for us are often delivered in a graded and progressive panorama, to allow our spirit the elasticity to accommodate the revelation if we are sufficiently attentive and surrendered to Him.

On this night, I woke up around 3:00 a.m. to use the restroom and afterwards was unable to go back to sleep. So, I lay in bed and sang spiritual songs until eventually I fell asleep.

In my dream, we were in a building where a minister of God conferred some spiritual authority upon us (me, Estella, and the kids). It was a little challenging for us (especially for me) as certain forces and elements around that place resisted what the minister of God was trying to do. But in the end, he prevailed, and we departed from that place.

When we came out of the building, a relative and her children joined us, and Estella drove the vehicle that we went in. While driving, I saw a very old big car with two men driving in it.

Suddenly, they passed us, stopped in the middle of the road, and came out. Having blocked our way, we were not able to go through. So, Estella made a detour by turning left to cut through the neighborhood and going in-between the clutter of houses, and we continued our journey. When I turned to look, I saw a woman by the roadside and some other people standing apart. So, I said to myself: "I hope those men will not harm the woman." Suddenly, instead of us in the vehicle, we were all walking by foot through a village. As we walked, I suddenly saw lots of silver coins strewn along the path we traveled. So, we all hastened to pick and gather up what we could. But, ultimately, along the way I dropped all of mine saying to myself that the local folks need it more than me. I saw that Estella also dropped hers. Few minutes later, we were all in a store and Estella offered to treat all of us with her card then I woke up again.

In the Gospel of John verses 9-11, we see that Jesus received a blessing at the river Jordan through the ministry of John the Baptist. Then straightaway we see that Jesus was beset in the wilderness by opposition from Satanic powers who were bent on creating a disruption to his ministry and his calling.

"12 Immediately the Spirit drove Him into the wilderness. 13 And He was there in the wilderness forty days, tempted by Satan, and was with the wild beasts; and the angels ministered to Him."

This is what happened in that dream when upon departing the place where God conferred upon us his blessing, these Satanic elements began to pursue me and my children. We have come under miscellaneous, mischievous, and callous attacks only because we want to serve God and do his work. People said all kinds of crazy things, including that we bought a church, etcetera. Simply because we chose to fulfil the obligation to serve God in the way and manner of our choosing. Just like in the dream, we have been pursued, waylaid, and hounded relentlessly for no other reason than our decision to obey God and serve Him in the way and manner of our choosing.

But the good thing in and through it all is that, as the angels came and ministered to Jesus in and through his trial, even so have we also experienced and witnessed the supernatural grace and salvation of God as borne out by finding abundant silver coin as we went on our way in the dream. And it is with that silver coin (that Divine blessing and empowerment) that we yield ourselves in the work of God to be a blessing to many. We also received promises from God of extraordinary Divine provision, which we can bear witness and attest that these things have surely come to pass. Amen.

SIX

ONE OF MANY
SPIRITUAL ATTACKS

A lot of times we have good intentions and fairly common plans. But we need to be careful, lest the devil use our routine, and typical tendencies and appetites to trick us out from a place of peace and protection into a place of entrapment.

The spiritual realms are very layered and represent a stack of vibrant and animated organic energies and forces that follow the designs and manipulations of people with bad intentions. Their plan is to harm us. Their plan is to lead us into compromise, into making decisions based on fake imagery and representations that lead us into a situation of entrapment, disadvantage, and sorrow.

"In this dream, I was traveling with a familiar travel partner (now deceased) and I asked where we were going. I told him I've already been to London, and he says the name of the place, so I spell out the name of a strange but exotic-sounding foreign country. I tell him I don't know the place. So now we are in the place and it's very bright... The skies are clear blue (at first) and we then fly into darkness, like nighttime. Then all of a sudden, we are walking behind the plane and the plane is taxiing in front of us to the runway. At this point, I am puzzled and wondering, "how can this be?... Why are we outside?" We were told that they are fixing the other landing space that's why we were diverted to this location. But I am still puzzled as to why we are outside of the plane (we are the only ones outside the plane).

We are now inside the airport, and we see people going down flights of stairs, but we are going up. We get to an elevator (since it's a foreign place we don't understand or read the language). There was board blocking the elevator, and I wasn't sure if it was there so that we don't use the elevator. But I moved it out of the way. There was a lady seated by the elevator. When I removed the board, the woman then motioned with her hand trying to tell me something, but I don't understand what the woman is trying to say. At this point, my travel partner is hesitant and does not get in the elevator, but I do, and I am now standing beside two other women. The elevator proceeds to go down. But when it comes to a stop we don't get out. One of the ladies then presses the button and the elevator proceeded back upwards. Then I awoke."

In this dream, I am willed and tricked into making a journey to a place of entrapment, based on my own appetite and love of travel. The devil has used imagery that will make me lower my guard and yield easily to a predetermined theater of entrapment. Only the grace of God and a sufficiency of prayers that have gone beforehand would see me through this trial and subterfuge.

Clearly, the presence of a familiar travel partner (now deceased) has put me in a vulnerable and disarming spiritual state. But from this point, everything plays out in a way that is both strange and suspicious: the travel destination is strange and suspicious; the way the skies turned from being bright and vibrant to being dark and gloomy in an instant as we made our descent to land at our destination was suspect; the manner by which we are disembarked or removed from the plane is suspicious --as though we had been smuggled into the country illegally or for underhand purposes.

And then seeing the melee of people descending downstairs when nobody was going up was a bad sign that this is a place of death and destruction; a place of entrapment. The communications were not forthcoming either, so that we were unable to communicate and figure out where to go and what to do.

We entered the elevator (ill-advisedly) to go up but instead went down to the very bottom. What saved me was that I did not go out from the elevator. I may not have been able to awake from this attack dream. And that could've been my end. A lot of people go to sleep at night and never wake up. This could've been one such night for me. But God sustained me.

By the grace of God, not being successful in tricking me into leaving the elevator, the elevator mechanism now started to go UP, which was my original destination --to extricate myself from this trap. And that is when I awoke, to the glory of God.

This dream was also a warning to me, to exercise judgment and be circumspect about opportunities that present themselves --be they travel or whatever. Not every shining opportunity is necessarily a good opportunity. Nor is it necessarily from God. Some blessings come from the devil, to tempt us. Because the devil knows what we like, and what we are prone to do and how we are likely to react when confronted with an opportunity. Especially, an opportunity that costs us little to nothing, but promises us excitement, fulfillment, and satisfaction of some kind.

The scriptures give us examples where Jesus was presented with opportunities which He turned down, but also which many of us might have taken up and pursued...

"When Jesus saw that they were ready to force him to be their king, he slipped away into the hills by himself." (John 6:15, NLT).

"23 Now when he was in Jerusalem at the Passover Feast, many believed in his name when they saw the signs that he was doing. 24 But Jesus on his part did not entrust himself to them, because he knew all people 25 and needed no one to bear witness about man, for he himself knew what was in man." (John 2:23-25, ESV).

"5 Then the devil took him to the holy city and had him stand on the highest point of the temple.

6 "If you are the Son of God," he said, "throw yourself down. For it is written: "'He will command his angels concerning you, and they will lift you up in their hands, so that you will not strike your foot against a stone.' " 7 Jesus answered him, "It is also written: 'Do not put the Lord your God to the test.' " (Matthew 4:5-7).

This dream also came at a time of great temptation in my life, and God was at work to help me prevail and come through the challenges victorious. The prayers of my church family and others availed for me in this trying period. I give God all the praise and glory.

Amen.

SEVEN

CERTIFICATION
OF HEALING

Recently, I went through a terrible spiritual struggle that resulted in me being absent from the church for several weeks. At the point where I was emerging from it all, and prior, to my being restored back to fellowship with the Saints in the House of God, I had three dreams where I received a miscellany of Heavenly messages that were unraveled, interpreted, and reinforced to me upon my arrival in church that Sunday. I will share the dreams and the conversation that resolved and explained them, putting them in context and perspective for me.

First Dream

I was on top of very high rocks from where I was surrounded by a few people. One of them dived down into the water while the others were just hanging around.

From my vantage point on the heights above, I could see clear to the ocean bottom below. I was scared because of the heights I was at. So, I decided I would descend to the embankment beneath. When I got there, I lathered my body with soap and was about to wash it off then I woke up.

Second Dream

I saw three children playing in the water. They were in a competition to see who could hold their breath under water the longest.

They eventually dispersed except one child who needed help getting out of the water. So, I helped the child come out and get safely to shore.

I was now going up the hill and came to a village, but no one was around at first. I saw a bundle of wood tied together and a stack of cassava leaf stems, as if someone was about to cook.

While looking around, I suddenly saw an older woman who came out to tell me about the village. Later, the older woman seemed to change in appearance and now looked like a chief of sorts in the village. She was carrying water in her hands and wanted me to wash my hands to go eat. I washed my hands and followed her but instead of eating food I was about to listen to the Word of God. I saw men dressed in choir uniform (blue and white collar) but instead of singing they just hung around while Apostle Etta was ministering, and later they left (while the preaching was still ongoing). I was wondering why they did not sing and just left.

Apostle Etta's preaching was extraordinary in the manner that it occurred. Instead of talking he was preaching in songs.

A familiar lady (I had a sense that I knew her by her voice) walked up holding a child, and she asked for Estella. I told her that Estella was about her father's business.

Walking along the river's embankment later, I saw many dead bodies. Then I woke up.

Third Dream

Since I was not able to sleep, I was urged to pray for the church and its members. I started praying for each member by name and God gave messages for some of them, which I was to deliver.

While still praying I dozed off and I saw that my house was stormed out by flood in a flash. Everything was lost. I stood in an empty house when suddenly I saw a short white man with shiny crown on his head entered followed by few other men.

One of them gave me a white duffel bag and the other one gave me a paper to sign, on which I did. The man stated that I was entitled to benefits.

The man with the crown on his head assured me that I wouldn't lack anything and that my benefits are intact.

From the conversation that occurred around these dreams, I was able to understand that God was certifying that his work of healing, deliverance, and salvation to recover me from my illness was being accelerated and that upon my return to the church (I had been missing for several weeks due to illness), He would complete the work of certification –which is what happened that Sunday. Before I even discussed the dreams with Apostle Etta, he came to me after the sermon and performed extensive prayers over me, and the elaborate but specific words he spoke described in detail the work that God was doing to certify my healing and recovery consistent with the dreams.

Evidently, there is washing and cleansing going

on (Dreams One and Two) to prepare me to be restored back to fellowship with the Saints (Dream Two) where I experienced the grace through the ministry of God's servant. Watching Apostle Etta preaching extensively and powerfully but by singing only and not speaking, was to convey to me the high prophetic nature of the ministration similar to what David and Asaph would do (i.e., both David and the Sons of Asaph ministered prophetically through song and not through speaking or talking and this is how the Psalms were developed).

This level of ministration is so pure that the professional and ceremonial ministries cannot fathom or abide, and this is why the ministers robed in blue and white could not join but only bore witness and then departed.

There was also a message for Estella, mirroring a situation in the Gospels when the family and community of Jesus were querying Him for being absent from the typical 'journey' that they would usually make together, and Jesus replied, "Why did you seek Me? Did you not know that I must be about My Father's business?" Then it says, "But they did not understand the statement which He spoke to them" (Luke 6:46-49).

And so, Estella should continue to be focused on the "Father's business", i.e., the work of God, and not be distracted to the left or to the right by anything or by anybody, group, family, or community.

There were many dead bodies along the river's embankment as a testament that we need to continue to be obedient to the LORD and His counsel, so that sudden death will not be our portion (and words by Apostle in his prayer for me before our conversation about the dreams later that day also spoke of death being removed from my physical frame, and God remolding my clay to formulate a new body for me, free from the signs and vestiges of death that had sought to claim me).

In Dream Three, it is a representation showing that all of that unsavory and undesirable experience (i.e., a sentence of death through my illness) had been washed away and stormed out, so that my house can be reconstituted and refurbished again, in line with the prayers). The angels provided the certification to me that my "benefits" from the LORD are intact, and He would reconstitute and refurbish me by His tender mercies and grace. Amen.

EIGHT

TEND YOUR SPIRITUAL HOUSE

In an effort to understand revelations better, the texture of dreams and visions, the way and manner they appear and manifest themselves, and better grasp their significance in our lives, I sought guidance. James 1:5 says:

"If any of you lack wisdom, let him ask of God, that giveth to all men liberally, and upbraideth not; and it shall be given him."

And so I sought guidance, and I will share with you the conversation that I was blessed with that threw some light on this. Hopefully, this will be a source of enlightenment to someone out there.

We are looking at and considering the spiritual firmament, construct or "house" that surrounds the space of every human being, every family, and every community, principality, or nation.

There is an array, swirl and vortex of spiritual energy that surrounds people, groups, and communities which takes its shape from the faith, habits, linkages, associations, contracts and covenants that people enter into and are a part of. Think of it like gravity. We know that living things have a certain gravitational aura and energy that they emanate, and which exerts a pull on other things, living and non-living.

And so larger objects such as moons, stars, planets, and also the sun, exert a pull against each other on the basis of their inherent gravitational energy. Hence, the universe is able to stay in a state of equilibrium with each planetary, sub-planetary, and extra-planetary orbital and their ecosystems remained in a state of balance relative to each other.

That is a crude analogy, but the fact remains that each person, family, community, and nation generate their own unique aura and energy signature, their own "house". And this is why we are warned in the scriptures against association with the ungodly, so that we do not become embroiled and entangled with the consequences of their unique energy signature --their spiritual "house".

"14 Be ye not unequally yoked together with unbelievers: for what fellowship hath righteousness with unrighteousness? and what communion hath light with darkness? 15 And what concord hath Christ with Belial? or what part hath he that believeth with an infidel?

16 And what agreement hath the temple of God with idols? for ye are the temple of the living God; as God hath said, I will dwell in them, and walk in them; and I will be their God, and they shall be my people.

17 Wherefore come out from among them, and be ye separate, saith the Lord, and touch not the unclean thing; and I will receive you" (2 Corinthians 6:14-17).

This is why, even after you have removed yourself from the company or from a contract or covenant with others --depending on a variety of factors, you may have the occasional dream where that person or persons still manifest in your spiritual space, in your spiritual "house", and constitute a snare to you. Because you had a linkage with them at some point that they have successfully, momentarily invoked --or due to a compromise by you, they have been able to momentarily exploit and invade your spiritual space. That is how and why they can enter your dreamscape (or spiritual "house") and tempt you.

Here are some additional examples of this spiritual house, that Jesus refers to as a "treasury" that each person has and from which the character, complexion and direction of their lives takes shape and form.

"34 You brood of vipers, how can you who are evil say anything good? For the mouth speaks what the heart is full of. 35 A good man brings good things out of the good stored up in him, and an evil man brings evil things out of the evil stored up in him"

(Matthew 12:34-35, NIV).

"43 "A good tree can't produce bad fruit, and a bad tree can't produce good fruit. 44 A tree is identified by its fruit. Figs are never gathered from thornbushes, and grapes are not picked from bramble bushes. 45 A good person produces good things from the treasury of a good heart, and an evil person produces evil things from the treasury of an evil heart. What you say flows from what is in your heart."

(Luke 6:43-45, NLT).

So, we all have this "treasury" or "store" or "house", which is like a virtual, parallel, space around us, and which mirrors the totality of our choices, actions, linkages, close friends and family. Essentially, a spiritual blend of the admixture of good or bad, or good and bad elements in the lives of those with whom we are tethered and connected. And this is why the choice of married partners is so important. And the choice of close friends and confidantes is so important. Is also why the choice of church we go to, and the choice of co-travelers in the journey of life is so very important. Because they affect the nature content and health of our spiritual "house"; hence, determining the types of dreams we have.

Let me give you a simple remedy: when your dreams become too complex for you to comprehend or get a handle on, take an inventory of all your linkages and associations, and review them from top to bottom. That is, those that are unimportant or that you cannot absolutely vouch for and can do without --drop at once. Recalibrate and reconstitute the matrix of relationships around you to conform to something more manageable and that you can vouch for on the basis of their alignment with God and with the Holy Spirit, and your dreams will gradually even out and streamline.

Initially, you may have some blowback and repercussions from severing ungodly relationships. But gradually, they will even out to where they are more manageable. And you will have a better understanding of the origins and meanings of certain dreams, because your spiritual "house" has been reorganized so that you can more easily identify what is an anomaly and what is an alien and foreign agent and element in your spiritual landscape.

ABOUT THE AUTHOR

Fanella Sampson is a grandmother, mother, mentor and Elder in the church mission of Spoken Word Faith Ministries based in Garland Texas. Gifted with many talents, she is also a writer and interior/event decorator. Her previous book: "How Great Thou Art" has been a blessing and inspiration to many. Ma Fanella as she is fondly called, currently lives in Dallas surrounded by a rich and vibrant community of family and friends.

Made in the USA
Monee, IL
27 February 2023